18

21

24

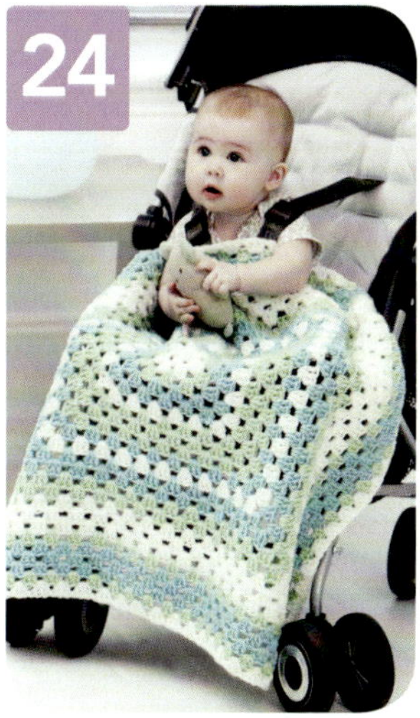

30

27

33

37

You CAN Do It!

Learn 1 Granny Square... Crochet 12 Projects!

We have used just one traditional crocheted granny throughout **this** book. So once you understand how this one square is made, you have the know-how to create any of the projects in this book.

More Squares = More Possibilities

x 1 =

x 2 =

x 4 =

If you like color & yarn, you'll love the many possibilities of the **Granny Square!**

Making a Granny

The granny is made of double crochets in groups of three. Each of these double crochet groups is called a shell. An extra shell and chains are worked at each of the four corners to give it a square shape.

To make this granny, you will need:

- Small amount of three colors of #4 medium weight yarn. (We used RED HEART® Super Saver® in 358 Lavender **A**, 321 Gold **B** and 886 Blue **C**.)
- Crochet hook 5.0 mm (US H-8)
- Small scissors
- Yarn needle
- Gauge or small ruler

The following stitches and techniques are used to make a granny square:

- Chain
- Join to form a ring
- Seaming
- Slip stitch
- Double crochet
- Weaving in ends

If you are not familiar with them you can learn more on the Red Heart website: redheart.com/learn

With **A**, chain 4, join with slip stitch in first chain to form ring.

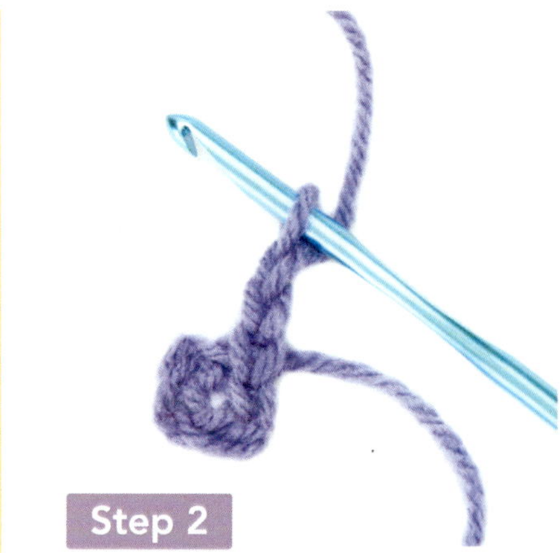

Chain 3; this counts as the first double crochet of your first round.

Work 2 double crochet into the ring. This completes the first 3-double crochet shell.

Chain 3, then do 3 double crochets into the ring. Repeat this two more times. Chain 3, join with a slip stitch to top of starting chain 3. You now have completed Round 1. It has four 3-double crochet shells and four chain-3 corners. Fasten off **A**.

For Round 2, with right side facing, join color **B** with a slip stitch in any corner chain-3 space; chain 3, (2 double crochet, chain 3, 3 double crochet) all in same chain-3 space; (3 double crochet, chain 3, 3 double crochet all in next chain-3 space) repeat what is in the parentheses a total of 3 times. Join with a slip stitch to top of starting chain 3. Round 2 has a total of eight 3-double crochet shells and four chain-3 corners. Fasten off **B**.

Making a Granny

Step 6

For Round 3, with right side facing, join **C** with slip stitch in any corner chain-3 space, chain 3, (2 double crochet, chain 3, 3 double crochet) all in same chain-3 space; (3 double crochet between next two 3-double crochet groups, 3 double crochet, chain 3, 3 double crochet all in next corner chain-3 space) 3 times, 3 double crochet between next two 3-double crochet groups, join with a slip stitch to top of starting chain 3.

Round 3 has a total of twelve 3-double crochet shells and four chain-3 corners. Fasten off **C**.

To make it easier, these instructions have spelled out many of the words that will be abbreviated in the patterns. When following patterns, refer to the Abbreviations list on page 41.

Step 7

For Round 4, with right side facing, join **A** with slip stitch in any corner chain-3 space, chain 3, (2 double crochet, chain 3, 3 double crochet) all in same chain-3 space, *(3 double crochet between next two 3-double crochet shells) twice, 3 double crochet, chain 3, 3 double crochet all in next corner chain-3 space, repeat from * twice more, (3 double crochet between next two 3-double crochet shells) twice, join with a slip stitch to top of starting chain 3. Round 4 has a total of sixteen 3-double crochet shells and four chain-3 corners. Fasten off **A**. Weave in all ends using a yarn needle.

Measure your finished square. If your gauge is correct it should measure 5" square. Since this is a practice square, gauge is not important. But when following a pattern in the book, be sure your square agrees with the gauge given with the pattern. If granny square is too large, try a smaller hook. If your square is too small, try a larger hook.

If you are making a square larger than this sample, continue to work each subsequent round the same as Round 4. Make sure to work a 3-double crochet shell in each space, and work the corners only in the chain-3 spaces of the previous corners.

Single Square Coasters

Begin your granny-making adventure by making grannies to use as coasters. Use a multi yarn for color interest, or make them in assorted solid colors to match with your décor.

Beginner

Finished Size
4" x 4"

Red Heart® Super Saver®
1 skein 996 French Country

Crochet Hook
5.0 mm [US H-8]

Gauge
Finished square measures 4" x 4".
CHECK YOUR GAUGE. Use any size hooks to obtain the gauge.

COASTER

Ch 4, join with a slip st in first ch to form a ring.

Round 1 (right side): Ch 3, 2 dc in ring, [ch 3, 3 dc in ring] 3 times, ch 3, join with a slip st in top of starting ch-3.

Round 2: Slip st in next 2 dc and ch-3 space, ch 3, (2 dc, ch 3, 3 dc) all in same ch-3 space, *(3 dc, ch 3, 3 dc) all in next ch-3 space; repeat from * twice, join with a slip st in top of starting ch-3.

Round 3: Slip st in next 2 dc and corner ch-3 space, ch 3, (2 dc, ch 3, 3 dc) all in same ch-3 space, *3 dc between next two 3-dc groups, (3 dc, ch 3, 3 dc) all in next corner ch 3 space; repeat from * twice, 3 dc between next two 3-dc groups, join with a slip st in top of starting ch-3. Fasten off. Weave in ends.

Two-Square Pincushion

Crochet two grannies, join them together with single crochets, and then stuff them with a little pillow—you'll have the perfect pincushion!

Beginner

Finished Size
5" x 5"

Red Heart® Super Saver®
1 skein each 321 Gold **A**, 319 Cherry Red **B**, and 631 Light Sage **C**

Notions
Two 6" fabric squares

Sewing needle and matching sewing thread

Small amount polyfill stuffing

Crochet Hook
5.0 mm [US H-8]

Gauge
Finished square measures 5" x 5".
CHECK YOUR GAUGE. Use any size hooks to obtain the gauge.

PINCUSHION

Square (make 2)

With **A**, ch 4, join with a slip st in first ch to form a ring.

Round 1 (right side): Ch 3, 2 dc in ring, [ch 3, 3 dc in ring] 3 times, ch 3, join with a slip st in top of starting ch-3. Fasten off **A**.

Round 2: With right side facing, join **B** with a slip st in any ch-3 space, ch 3, (2 dc, ch 3, 3 dc) all in same ch-3 space, *(3 dc, ch 3, 3 dc) all in next ch-3 space; repeat from * twice, join with a slip st in top of starting ch-3. Fasten off **B**.

Round 3: With right side facing, join **C** with a slip st in any corner ch-3 space, ch 3, (2 dc, ch 3, 3 dc) all in same ch-3 space, *3 dc between next two 3-dc groups, (3 dc, ch 3, 3 dc) all in next corner ch-3 space; repeat from * twice, 3 dc between next two 3-dc groups, join with a slip st in top of starting ch-3. Fasten off **C**.

Round 4: With right side facing, join **A** with a slip st in any corner ch-3 space, ch 3, (2 dc, ch 3, 3 dc) all in same ch-3 space, *[3 dc between next two 3-dc groups] twice, (3 dc, ch 3, 3 dc) all in next corner ch-3 space; repeat from * twice, [3 dc between next two 3-dc groups] twice, join with a slip st in top of starting ch-3. Fasten off **A**. Weave in ends.

Assembly

Place fabric squares right sides together; with sewing needle and thread, sew a ½" seam leaving an opening for turning. Trim corners and turn right side out, stuff with fiberfill and sew opening closed.

Holding both crochet squares with wrong sides facing and working through both squares at the same time, join **A** with a slip st in any corner ch-3 space, ch 1, 3 sc in corner ch-3 space, *sc in next 12 dc, 3 sc in next corner ch-3 space; repeat from * twice. Insert stuffed square into crocheted cover, sc in next 12 dc, join with a slip st in first sc. Fasten off. Weave in ends.

Four-Square Cowl

You'll need just four grannies to make this easy cowl to keep your neck warm. Of course, you can add squares if you'd like a longer cowl.

Beginner

Finished Size
24" circumference x 6" wide

Red Heart® Super Saver®
1 skein each 313 Aran **A**, 661 Frosty Green **B**, 886 Blue **C**, and 400 Grey Heather **D**

Crochet Hook
6.5 mm [US K-11]

Gauge
First 3 rounds of square measures 4¾" across. Finished square measures 6" x 6". **CHECK YOUR GAUGE. Use any size hooks to obtain the gauge.**

Color Pattern
Make one square in each of the following color combinations:
Square 1: Rounds 1 & 2 **A**, Round 3 **B**, Round 4 **D**
Square 2: Rounds 1 & 2 **C**, Round 3 **A**, Round 4 **D**
Square 3: Rounds 1 & 2 **B**, Round 3 **A**, Round 4 **D**
Square 4: Round 1 **A**, Round 2 & 3 **C**, Round 4 **D**

COWL

Square
With first color, ch 4, join with a slip st in first ch to form a ring.
Round 1 (right side): Ch 3, 2 dc in ring, [ch 3, 3 dc in ring] 3 times, ch 3, join with a slip st in top of starting ch-3. Fasten off if changing color.
Round 2: Slip st in next 2 dc and ch-3 space or join next color with slip st in any ch-3 space, ch 3, (2 dc, ch 3, 3 dc) all in same ch-3 space, *(3 dc, ch 3, 3 dc) all in next ch-3 space); repeat from * twice, join with a slip st in top of starting ch-3. Fasten off if changing color.
Round 3: Slip st in next 2 dc and corner ch-3 space or with right side facing, join next color with slip st in any corner ch-3 space, ch 3, (2 dc, ch 3, 3 dc) all in same ch-3 space, *3 dc between next two 3-dc groups, (3 dc, ch 3, 3 dc) all in next corner ch-3 space; repeat from * twice, 3 dc between next two 3-dc groups, join with a slip st in top of starting ch-3. Fasten off.

Round 4: With right side facing, join **D** with a slip st in any corner ch-3 space, ch 3, (2 dc, ch 3, 3 dc) all in same ch-3 space, *[3 dc between next two 3-dc groups] twice, (3 dc, ch 3, 3 dc) all in next corner ch-3 space; repeat from * twice, [3 dc between next two 3-dc groups] twice, join with a slip st in top of starting ch-3. Fasten off **D**. Weave in ends.

Assembly
With matching color yarn, holding right sides together, whipstitch squares together through back loops only, in the following order: Square 1 to Square 2, Square 2 to Square 3, Square 3 to Square 4. Then join Square 4 to Square 1 to form a tube. Weave in ends.

Nine-Square Scarf

We've used five colors for this nine-square warmer, but you can use as many or as few colors as you like. Use the same color for the last round of all nine grannies to tie the color scheme together.

Beginner

Finished Size
7½" x 65"

Red Heart® Super Saver®
1 skein each 321 Gold **A**, 886 Blue **B**, 376 Burgundy **C**, 358 Lavender **D**, and 312 Black **E**

Crochet Hook
6.0 mm [US J-10]

Gauge
First 3 rounds of square measures 4½" across. Finished square measures 7" x 7". **CHECK YOUR GAUGE. Use any size hooks to obtain the gauge.**

Color Pattern

Make one square in each of the following color combinations:

Square 1: 1 round each **A**, **B**, **C**, **A**, **E**
Square 2: 1 round each **A**, **C**, **D**, **B**, **E**
Square 3: 1 round each **C**, **D**, **A**, **C**, **E**
Square 4: 1 round each **C**, **A**, **B**, **D**, **E**
Square 5: 1 round each **C**, **B**, **D**, **C**, **E**
Square 6: 1 round each **B**, **D**, **A**, **C**, **E**
Square 7: 1 round each **D**, **A**, **B**, **D**, **E**
Square 8: 1 round each **D**, **B**, **C**, **A**, **E**
Square 9: 1 round each **B**, **C**, **D**, **B**, **E**

SCARF

Square

With first color, ch 4, join with slip st in first ch to form a ring.

Round 1 (right side): Ch 3, 2 dc in ring, [ch 3, 3 dc in ring] 3 times, ch 3, join with a slip st in top of starting ch-3. Fasten off.

Round 2: With right side facing, join next color with a slip st in any ch-3 space, ch 3, (2 dc, ch 3, 3 dc) all in same ch-3 space, *(3 dc, ch 3, 3 dc) all in next ch-3 space); repeat from * twice, join with a slip st in top of starting ch-3. Fasten off.

Round 3: With right side facing, join next color with a slip st in any corner ch-3 space, ch 3, (2 dc, ch 3, 3 dc) all in same ch-3 space, *3 dc between next two 3-dc groups, (3 dc, ch 3, 3 dc) all in next corner ch-3 space; repeat from * twice, 3 dc between next two 3-dc groups, join with a slip st in top of starting ch-3. Fasten off.

Round 4: With right side facing, join next color with a slip st in any corner ch-3 space, ch 3, (2 dc, ch 3, 3 dc) all in same ch-3 space, *[3 dc between next two 3-dc groups] twice, (3 dc, ch 3, 3 dc) all in next corner ch-3 space, repeat from * twice, [3 dc between next two 3-dc groups] twice, join with a slip st in top of starting ch-3. Fasten off.

Round 5: With right side facing, join **E** with a slip st in any corner ch-3 space, ch 3, (2 dc, ch 3, 3 dc) all in same ch-3 space, *[3 dc between next two 3-dc groups] 3 times, (3 dc, ch 3, 3 dc) all in next corner ch-3 space; repeat from * twice, [3 dc between next two 3-dc groups] 3 times, join with a slip st in top of starting ch-3. Fasten off **E**. Weave in ends.

Assembly

Place squares in order from Square 1 to Square 9. With **E**, holding right sides together, whipstitch squares into a single row.

Border

With right side facing, join **E** with a slip st in any corner ch-3 space, ch 1, *3 sc in corner ch-3 space, sc in each dc and ch-space across to next corner ch-3 space; repeat from * around; join with a slip st in first sc. Fasten off. Weave in ends.

Two-Square Pillow

Crochet two larger squares, join their edges together with single crochet, add a pillow form and finish the edge—you have an easy-care pillow that will add comfort to your world.

Beginner

Finished Size
16" x 16" without flange

Red Heart® Super Saver®
1 skein each 334 Buff **A**, 928 Earth & Sky **B**, 505 Aruba Sea **C**, and 360 Cafe **D**

Notions
16" pillow form

Crochet Hook
6.0 mm [US J-10]

Gauge
First 3 rounds of square measures 4½" across. **CHECK YOUR GAUGE. Use any size hooks to obtain the gauge.**

PILLOW

Square (make 2)
With **A**, ch 4, join with slip st in first ch to form ring.
Round 1 (right side): Ch 3, 2 dc in ring, [ch 3, 3 dc in ring] 3 times, ch 3, join with a slip st to top of starting ch-3.

Round 2: Slip st in next 2 dc and ch-3 space, ch 3, (2 dc, ch 3, 3 dc) all in same ch-3 space, *(3 dc, ch 3, 3 dc) all in next ch-3 space; repeat from * twice, join with a slip st in top of starting ch-3.

Round 3: Slip st in next 2 dc and corner ch-3 space, ch 3, (2 dc, ch 3, 3 dc) all in same ch-3 space, *3 dc between next two 3-dc groups, (3 dc, ch 3, 3 dc) all in next corner ch-3 space; repeat from * twice, 3 dc between next two 3-dc groups, join with a slip st in top of starting ch-3. Fasten off **A**.

Round 4: Join **B** with slip st in any corner ch-3 space, ch 3, (2 dc, ch 3, 3 dc) all in same ch-3 space, *[3 dc between next two 3-dc groups] twice, (3 dc, ch 3, 3 dc) all in next corner ch-3 space, repeat from * twice, [3 dc between next two 3-dc groups] twice, join with a slip st in top of starting ch-3.

Round 5: Slip st in next 2 dc and in corner ch-3 space, ch 3, (2 dc, ch 3, 3 dc) all in same ch-3 space, *[3 dc between next two 3-dc groups] across to next corner, (3 dc, ch 3, 3 dc) all in next corner ch-3 space; repeat from * twice, [3 dc between next two 3-dc groups] across to next corner, join with a slip st in top of starting ch-3.

Round 6: Repeat Round 5, increasing one 3-dc group on each side of square. Fasten off **B**.

Rounds 7-9: Change to **C** and repeat Rounds 4-6, increasing one 3-dc group on each side of square on each round. At the end of round 9, fasten off **C**.

Rounds 10-12: Change to **D** and repeat Rounds 4-6, increasing one 3-dc group on each side of square on each round. At the end of round 12, fasten off. Weave in ends.

Assembly/Flange

Round 1: Holding both squares together with wrong sides together, and working through double thickness, join **D** with a slip st in any corner ch-3 space, ch 1, *3 sc in corner ch-3 space, sc in next 36 dc*; repeat from * to * twice, insert pillow form into crocheted cover, repeat from * to * once, join with slip st in first sc.

Round 2: Ch 1, sc in same sc as slip st, *3 sc in next sc, sc in next 38 sc; repeat from * twice, 3 sc in next sc, sc in next 37 sc, join with a slip st to first sc.

Round 3: Ch 1, sc in same sc as slip st, sc in next sc, *3 sc in next sc, sc in next 40 sc; repeat from * twice, 3 sc in next sc, sc in next 38sc, join with a slip st to first sc. Fasten off. Weave in ends.

Six-by-Six Blanket

Ready for a larger project that baby will enjoy from newborn days through toddler years? This 36 square project is a wonderful shower gift to welcome baby.

Beginner

Finished Size
37" x 37" square

Red Heart® Super Saver®
2 skeins 373 Petal Pink **C**
1 skein each 381 Lt Blue **A**, 995 Ocean **B**, and 505 Aruba Sea **D**

Crochet Hook
6.5 mm [US K-11]

Gauge
First 3 rounds of square measures 4¾" across. Finished square measures 6" x 6". **CHECK YOUR GAUGE. Use any size hooks to obtain the gauge.**

BLANKET

Square

(make 9 in each color, 36 total)

Ch 4, join with slip st in first ch to form ring.

Round 1 (right side): Ch 3, 2 dc in ring, [ch 3, 3 dc in ring] 3 times, ch 3, join with a slip st in top of starting ch-3.

Round 2: Slip st next 2 dc and corner ch-3 space, ch 3, (2 dc, ch 3, 3 dc) all in same ch-3 space, *(3 dc, ch 3, 3 dc) all in next ch-3 space; repeat from * twice, join with a slip st in top of starting ch-3.

Round 3: Slip st in next 2 dc and corner ch 3 space, ch 3, (2 dc, ch 3, 3 dc) all in same ch-3 space, *3 dc between next two 3-dc groups, (3 dc, ch 3, 3 dc) all in next corner ch-3 space; repeat from * twice, 3 dc between next two 3-dc groups, join with a slip st in top of starting ch-3.

Round 4: Slip st in next 2 dc and corner ch 3 space, ch 3, (2 dc, ch 3, 3 dc) all in same ch-3 space, *[3 dc between next two 3-dc groups] twice, (3 dc, ch 3, 3 dc) all in next corner ch-3 space, repeat from * twice, [3 dc between next two 3-dc groups] twice, join with a slip st in top of starting ch-3. Fasten off. Weave in ends.

Assembly

With matching color yarn, holding right sides together, whipstitch squares together into six strips of six squares each, following **Assembly Diagram**. Whipstitch strips together in same manner.

continued

Six-by-Six Blanket

Border

Round 1: With right side facing, join **C** with a slip st in any corner ch-3 space, ch 1, *3 sc in corner ch-3 space, [sc in next 12 dc, sc in next ch-space, sc in joining, sc in next ch-space] 5 times, sc in next 12 dc; repeat from * around, join with a slip st to first sc of round. Fasten off **C**.

Round 2: With right side facing, join **B** with a slip st in any corner sc, ch 1, *3 sc in corner sc, sc in each sc across to next corner; repeat from * around, join with a slip st in first sc. Fasten off.

D	C	D	B	C	A
C	D	B	C	A	B
D	B	C	A	B	D
B	C	A	B	D	A
C	A	B	D	A	C
A	B	D	A	C	D

ASSEMBLY DIAGRAM

Five-by-Five Throw

By making grannies 11 inches square, you only have to crochet 25 grannies for this eye-catching throw. Grab your hook and 6 colors of yarn and you're on your way to having a relaxing granny throw.

Beginner

Finished Size
55" x 55" square without border

Red Heart® Super Saver®
3 skeins 334 Buff **A**
2 skeins each 305 Aspen Print **D** and 631 Light Sage **E**
1 skein each 360 Cafe **B**, 661 Frosty Green **C**, 656 Real Teal **F**

Crochet Hook
6.0 mm [US J-10]

Gauge
First 3 rounds of square measures 4½" across. Finished square measures 11" x 11". **CHECK YOUR GAUGE. Use any size hooks to obtain the gauge.**

Color Pattern
Make designated number of squares in each of the following color combinations:
Square 1 (make 5): Rounds 1 & 2 **D**, Round 3 **A**, Round 4 **F**, Rounds 5 & 6 **A**, Round 7 **E**, Round 8 **A**
Square 2 (make 8): Rounds 1 & 2 **F**, Round 3 **A**, Round 4 **E**, Rounds 5 & 6 **B**, Round 7 **F**, Round 8 **A**
Square 3 (make 8): Rounds 1 & 2 **B**, Round 3 **C**, Round 4 **A**, Rounds 5 & 6 **E**, Round 7 **D**, Round 8 **A**
Square 4 (make 4): Rounds 1 & 2 **C**, Round 3 **B**, Round 4 **E**, Rounds 5 & 6 **D**, Round 7 **C**, Round 8 **A**

THROW

Square

With first color, ch 4, join with slip st in first ch to form a ring.
Round 1 (right side): Ch 3, 2 dc in ring, [ch 3, 3 dc in ring] 3 times, ch 3, join with a slip st in top of starting ch-3.

Round 2: Slip st in next 2 dc and ch-3 space, ch 3, (2 dc, ch 3, 3 dc) all in same ch-3 space, *(3 dc, ch 3, 3 dc) all in next ch-3 space; repeat from * twice, join with a slip st in top of starting ch-3. Fasten off.

Round 3: With right side facing, join next color with a slip st in any corner ch-3 space, ch 3, (2 dc, ch 3, 3 dc) all in same ch-3 space, *3 dc between next two 3-dc groups, (3 dc, ch 3, 3 dc) all in next corner ch-3 space; repeat from *

continued

twice, 3 dc between next two 3-dc groups, join with a slip st in top of starting ch-3. Fasten off.

Round 4: With right side facing, join next color with a slip st in any corner ch-3 space, ch 3, (2 dc, ch 3, 3 dc) all in same ch-3 space, *[3 dc between next two 3-dc groups] twice, (3 dc, ch 3, 3 dc) all in next corner ch-3 space, repeat from * twice, [3 dc between next two 3-dc groups] twice, join with a slip st in top of starting ch-3. Fasten off.

Round 5: With right side facing, join next color with a slip st in any corner ch-3 space, ch 3, (2 dc, ch 3, 3 dc) all in same ch-3 space, *[3 dc between next two 3-dc groups] 3 times, (3 dc, ch 3, 3 dc) all in next corner ch-3 space; repeat from * twice, [3 dc between next two 3-dc groups] 3 times, join with a slip st in top of starting ch-3.

Round 6: Slip st in next 2 dc and corner ch-3 space, ch 3, (2 dc, ch 3, 3 dc) all in same ch-3 space, *[3 dc between next two 3-dc groups] 4 times, (3 dc, ch 3, 3 dc) all in next corner ch-3 space; repeat from * twice, [3 dc between next two 3-dc groups] 4 times, join with a slip st in top of starting ch-3. Fasten off.

Round 7: With right side facing, join next color with a slip st in any corner ch-3 space, ch 3, (2 dc, ch 3, 3 dc) all in same ch-3 space, *[3 dc between next two 3-dc groups] 5 times, (3 dc, ch 3, 3 dc) all in next corner ch-3 space; repeat from * twice, [3 dc between next two 3-dc groups] 5 times, join with a slip st in top of starting ch-3. Fasten off.

Round 8: With right side facing, join **A** with a slip st in any corner ch-3 space, ch 3, (2 dc, ch 3, 3 dc) all in same ch-3 space, *[3 dc between next two 3-dc groups] 6 times, (3 dc, ch 3, 3 dc) all in next corner ch-3 space; repeat from * twice, [3 dc between next two 3-dc groups] 6 times, join with a slip st in top of starting ch-3. Fasten off **A**. Weave in ends.

Assembly

Arrange squares following **Assembly Diagram**. With **A** and holding right sides together, whipstitch squares together into five strips of five squares each. Whipstitch strips together in same manner.

Border

Round 1: With right side facing, join **A** with a slip st in any corner ch-3 space, ch 3, (2 dc, ch 3, 3 dc) all in same ch-3 space, *[(3 dc between next two 3-dc groups) 7 times, 3 dc in next 2 ch-3 spaces] 4 times, [3 dc between next two 3-dc groups] 7 times, (3 dc, ch 3, 3 dc) all in next corner ch-3 space; repeat from * around, ending last repeat at **, join with a slip st in top of starting ch-3.

Round 2: Slip st in next 2 dc and corner ch-3 space, (2 dc, ch 3, 3 dc) all in same ch-3 space, *[3 dc between next two 3-dc groups] 44 times, (3 dc, ch 3, 3 dc) all in next corner ch-3 space; repeat from * twice, [3 dc between next two 3-dc groups] 44 times, join with a slip st in top of starting ch-3. Fasten off. Weave in ends.

1	3	2	3	1
3	2	4	2	3
2	4	1	4	2
3	2	4	2	3
1	3	2	3	1

ASSEMBLY DIAGRAM

One Square Travel Blankie

Here's a blanket that is sized for a car seat or stroller. You start this big square in the center (just like any other granny) and then just keep adding rounds.

Beginner

Finished Size
28" x 28" square

Red Heart® Super Saver®
1 skein each 316 Soft White , 668 Honeydew , and 505 Aruba Sea

Crochet Hook
5.5 mm [US I-9]

Gauge
First 3 rounds of square measures 4¼" across.

Color Pattern

Work Blankie in the following color sequence:
Rounds 1 & 2 - **A**
Round 3 - **B**
Rounds 4 & 5 - **C**
Round 6 - **A**
Rounds 7, 8 & 9 - **B**
Round 10 - **C**
Round 11 - **A**
Rounds 12 & 13 - **C**
Rounds 14 & 15 - **B**
Rounds 16, 17 & 18 - **A**
Round 19 - **B**
Rounds 20, 21 & 22 - **C**
Round 23 - **B**
Round 24 - **A**

BLANKIE

With **A**, ch 4, join with slip st in first ch to form a ring.
Round 1 (right side): Ch 3, 2 dc in ring, [ch 3, 3 dc in ring] 3 times, ch 3, join with a slip st in top of starting ch-3.

Round 2: Slip st in next 2 dc and next ch-3 space, ch 3, (2 dc, ch 3, 3 dc) all in same ch-3 space, *(3 dc, ch 3, 3 dc) all in next ch-3 space; repeat from * twice, join with a slip st in top of starting ch-3. Fasten off **A**.

Round 3: With right side facing, join **B** with a slip st in any corner ch-3 space, ch 3, (2 dc, ch 3, 3 dc) all in same ch-3 space, *3 dc between next two 3-dc groups, (3 dc, ch 3, 3 dc) all in next corner ch-3 space; repeat from * twice, 3 dc between next two 3-dc groups, join with a slip st in top of starting ch-3. Fasten off **B**.

Round 4: With right side facing, join **C** with a slip st in any corner ch-3 space, ch 3, (2 dc, ch 3, 3 dc) all in same ch-3 space, *[3 dc between next two 3-dc groups] twice, (3 dc, ch 3, 3 dc) all in next corner ch-3 space, repeat from * twice, [3 dc between next two 3-dc groups] twice, join with a slip st in top of starting ch-3.

Round 5: Slip st in next 2 dc and in corner ch-3 space or join next color with slip st in any corner ch-3 space, ch 3, (2 dc, ch 3, 3 dc) all in same ch-3 space, *[3 dc between next two 3-dc groups] across to next corner, (3 dc, ch 3, 3 dc) all in next corner ch-3 space; repeat from * twice, [3 dc between next two 3-dc groups] across to next corner, join with a slip st in top of starting ch-3. Fasten off if changing color.

Rounds 6-24: Maintaining color sequence as established, repeat Round 5, increasing one 3-dc group on each side of square on each round. At the end of Round 24, fasten off. Weave in ends.

Two-Size-Squares Throw

When some grannies are two times the size of other grannies, they can be stitched together in new creative ways. This throw was done in shades to please an outdoorsy nature lover.

Beginner

Finished Size
54" x 54" square

Red Heart® Super Saver®
5 skeins of 971 Camouflage **A**
2 skeins each of 334 Buff **B** and 360 Cafe **C**
1 skein of 631 Light Sage **D**

Crochet Hook
5.5 mm [US I-9]

Gauge
First 3 rounds of square measures 4¼" across. Finished small square measures 8" x 8"; large square measures 16" x 16". **CHECK YOUR GAUGE. Use any size hook to obtain the gauge.**

THROW

Large Solid Square (make 5)

With **A**, ch 4, join with slip st in first ch to form a ring.

Round 1 (right side): Ch 3, 2 dc in ring, [ch 3, 3 dc in ring] 3 times, ch 3, join with a slip st to top of starting ch-3.

Round 2: Slip st in next 2 dc and ch-3 space, ch 3, (2 dc, ch 3, 3 dc) all in same ch-3 space, *(3 dc, ch 3, 3 dc) all in next ch-3 space; repeat from * twice, join with a slip st in top of starting ch-3.

Round 3: Slip st in next 2 dc and corner ch-3 space, ch 3, (2 dc, ch 3, 3 dc) all in same ch-3 space, *3 dc between next two 3-dc groups, (3 dc, ch 3, 3 dc) all in next corner ch-3 space; repeat from * twice, 3 dc between next two 3-dc groups, join with a slip st in top of starting ch-3.

Round 4: Slip st in next 2 dc and corner ch-3 space, ch 3, (2 dc, ch 3, 3 dc) all in same ch-3 space, *[3 dc between next two 3-dc groups] across to next corner, (3 dc, ch 3, 3 dc) all in next corner ch-3 space, repeat from * twice, [3 dc between next two 3-dc groups] across to next corner, join with a slip st in top of starting ch-3.

Rounds 5-13: Repeat Round 4, increasing one 3-dc group on each side of square on each round. At the end of round 13, fasten off. Weave in ends.

Round 14: With right side facing, join **B** with a slip st in any corner ch-3 space, ch 1, *3 sc in corner ch-3 space, sc in each dc to next corner ch-3 space; repeat from * around, join with a slip st in first sc. Fasten off **B**.

Small Square Color Patterns

Make designated number of Small Squares in each of the following color combinations:
Square 1 (make 3): Round 1 & 2 **C**, Rounds 3, 4, & 5 **D**, Round 6 **B**.
Square 2 (make 3): Round 1 & 2 **C**, Rounds 3, 4, & 5 **B**, Round 6 **D**.
Square 3 (make 3): Round 1 & 2 **D**, Rounds 3 & 4 **B**, Rounds 5 & 6 **C**.
Square 4 (make 3): Round 1 **D**, Rounds 2 & 3 **C**, Rounds 4, 5 & 6 **B**.
Square 5 (make 2): Rounds 1, 2, & 3 **B**, Round 4 **C**, Rounds 5 & 6 **D**

continued

Two-Size-Squares Throw

Square 6 (make 2): Round 1 & 2 **B**, Round 3 **D**, Rounds 4, 5 & 6 **C**.

Small Square

With first color, ch 4, join with slip st in first ch to form ring.

Round 1 (right side): Ch 3, 2 dc in ring, [ch 3, 3 dc in ring] 3 times, ch 3, join with a slip st in top of starting ch-3. Fasten off if changing colors.

Round 2: Slip st in next 2 dc and ch-3 space or join next color with slip st in any ch-3 space, ch 3, (2 dc, ch 3, 3 dc) all in same ch-3 space, *(3 dc, ch 3, 3 dc) all in next ch-3 space); repeat from * twice, join with a slip st in top of starting ch-3. Fasten off if changing color.

Round 3: Slip st in next 2 dc and ch-3 space or join next color with slip st in any ch-3 space, ch 3, (2 dc, ch 3, 3 dc) all in same ch-3 space, *3 dc between next two 3-dc groups, (3 dc, ch 3, 3 dc) all in next corner ch-3 space; repeat from * twice, 3 dc between next two 3-dc groups, join with a slip st in top of starting ch-3. Fasten off if changing color.

Round 4: Slip st in next 2 dc and ch-3 space or join next color with slip st in any ch-3 space, ch 3, (2 dc, ch 3, 3 dc) all in same ch-3 space, *[3 dc between next two 3-dc groups] across to next corner, (3 dc, ch 3, 3 dc) all in next corner ch-3 space, repeat from * twice, [3 dc between next two 3-dc groups] across to next corner, join with a slip st in top of starting ch-3. Fasten off if changing color.

Rounds 5-6: Repeat round 4, increasing one 3-dc group on each side of square on each round. At the end of round 6, fasten off. Weave in ends.

Assemble Small Squares

Arrange small squares into 4 groups of 4 squares each, following **Assembly Diagram**. With right sides together, using matching color yarn, whipstitch each group of 4 small squares into one Large Combination Square. There are now 4 Large Combination Squares.

Combination Square Border

Work on each of the Large Combination Squares.

Round 1: With right side facing, join **B** with a slip st in any corner ch-3 space, ch 1, *3 sc in corner ch-3 space, sc in each of next 18 dc, 3 sc in each of next 2 ch-3 spaces, sc in each of next 18 dc; repeat from * around, join with a slip st in first sc. Fasten off **B**.

Assembly

Arrange large squares according to **Assembly Diagram** and, with right sides together, whipstitch into three strips of three large squares each. Whipstitch strips together in same manner.

Border

Round 1: With right side facing, join **B** with a slip st in center sc of any corner 3-sc group, ch 1, *3 sc in corner sc, sc in each sc and ch-space to center sc of next corner 3-sc group; repeat from * around, join with slip st in first sc.

Round 2: Ch 1, sc in same sc as joining, *3 sc in next corner sc, sc in each sc across to next corner sc; repeat from * around, join with a slip st in first sc. Fasten off **B**.

Round 3: With right side facing, join **C** with a slip st in center sc of any corner 3-sc group, ch 3, 2 dc in same st, *dc in each sc across to next corner sc, 3 dc in next corner sc; repeat from * twice, dc in each sc to beginning of round, join with a slip st in top of starting ch-3.

Round 4: Ch 3, *3 dc in next dc, dc in each dc to next corner; repeat from * around, join with a slip st in top of starting ch-3. Fasten off **C**.

Round 5: With right side facing, join **A** with a slip st in center dc of any corner 3-dc group, ch 1, *3 sc in corner sc, sc in each dc across to next corner, repeat from * around, join with a slip st in first sc.

Round 6: Ch 1, sc in first sc, *3 sc in next sc, sc in each dc across to next corner, repeat from * around, join with a slip st in first sc.

Round 7: Ch 1, sc in first sc, sc in next sc, *3 sc in next corner sc, sc in each dc across to next corner, repeat from * around, join with a slip st in first sc. Fasten off **A**. Weave in ends.

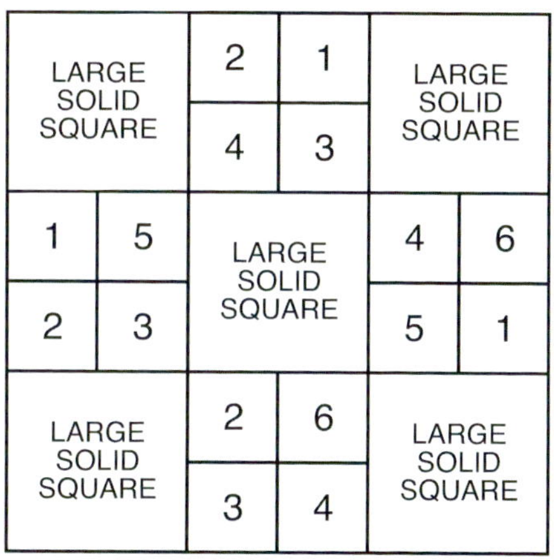

ASSEMBLY DIAGRAM

One Big Granny Throw

Crochet this interesting take on the granny by starting in the center with a multi-colored yarn and working out toward the edges. Then add a bit of drama with border rounds of three coordinating solid colors.

Beginner

Finished Size
47" x 47" square

Red Heart® Super Saver®
3 skeins of 310 Monet **A**
1 skein each 661 Frosty Green **B**, 358 Lavender **C**, and 631 Light Sage **D**

Crochet Hook
6.0 mm [US J-10]

Gauge
First 3 rounds of square measures 4½" across. **CHECK YOUR GAUGE. Use any size hooks to obtain the gauge.**

THROW

With **A**, ch 4, join with slip st in first ch to form a ring.
Round 1 (right side): Ch 3, 2 dc in ring, [ch 3, 3 dc in ring] 3 times, ch 3, join with a slip st in top of starting ch-3.
Round 2: Slip st in next 2 dc and ch-3 space, ch 3 (2 dc, ch 3, 3 dc) all in same ch-3 space, *(3 dc, ch 3, 3 dc) all in next ch-3 space; repeat from * twice, join with a slip st in top of starting ch-3.
Round 3: Slip st in next 2 dc and corner ch-3 space, ch 3 (2 dc, ch 3, 3 dc) all in same ch-3 space, *3 dc between next two 3-dc groups, (3 dc, ch 3, 3 dc) all in next corner ch-3 space; repeat from * twice, 3 dc between next two 3-dc groups, join with a slip st in top of starting ch-3.
Round 4: Slip st in next 2 dc and corner ch-3 space, ch 3, (2 dc, ch 3, 3 dc) all in same ch-3 space, *[3 dc between next two 3-dc groups] across to next corner, (3 dc, ch 3, 3 dc) all in next corner ch-3 space; repeat from * twice, [3 dc between next two 3-dc groups] across to next corner, join with a slip st in top of starting ch-3.
Rounds 5-29: Repeat Round 4, increasing one 3-dc group on each side of square on each round. At the end of round 29, fasten off.

Borders

Round 30: With right side facing, join **B** with a slip st in any corner ch-3 space, ch 3, (2 dc, ch 3, 3 dc) all in same ch-3 space, *[3 dc between next two 3-dc groups] across to next corner, (3 dc, ch 3, 3 dc) all in next corner ch-3 space; repeat from * twice, [3 dc between next two 3-dc groups] across to next corner, join with a slip st in top of starting ch-3.

Rounds 31-32: Slip st in next 2 dc and corner ch-3 space, ch 3, (2 dc, ch 3, 3 dc) all in same ch-3 space, *[3 dc between next two 3-dc groups] across to next corner, (3 dc, ch 3, 3 dc) all in next corner ch-3 space; repeat from * twice, [3 dc between next two 3-dc groups] across to next corner, join with a slip st in top of starting ch-3. At the end of Round 32, fasten off **B**.

Rounds 33-35: Repeat rounds 30-32, working all 3 rounds with **C**.

Rounds 36-38: Repeat rounds 30-32, working 3 rounds with **D**.

Fasten off. Weave in ends.

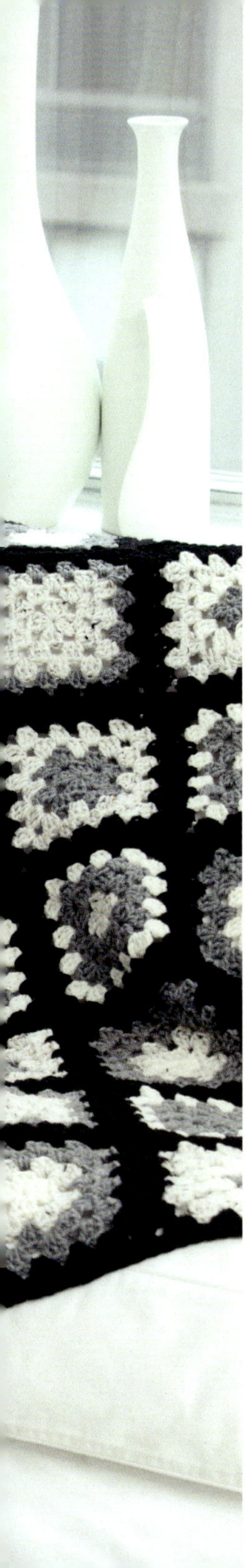

Seven-by-Eight Throw

If you're looking for a more sophisticated urban style, crochet this throw in high contrast shades as shown. Of course, you can adapt this throw to your own color preferences and wrap yourself in your personal colors of choice.

Beginner

Finished Size
49" wide x 56" long

Red Heart® Super Saver®
3 skeins 312 Black **D**
2 skeins each 400 Grey Heather **B**, and 4313 Aran Fleck **C**
1 skein 313 Aran **A**

Crochet Hook
6.0 mm [US J-10]

Gauge
First 3 rounds of square measures 4½" across. Finished square measures 7" x 7". **CHECK YOUR GAUGE. Use any size hooks to obtain the gauge.**

Color Pattern
Make 7 squares in each of the following color combinations (total 56):
Square 1: Round 1 **A**, Round 2 **C**, Rounds 3 & 4 **B**, Round 5 **D**
Square 2: Rounds 1, 2 & 3 **C**, Round 4 **B**, Round 5 **D**
Square 3: Round 1 **C**, Rounds 2 & 3 **B**, Round 4 **A**, Round 5 **D**
Square 4: Rounds 1 & 2 **C**, Round 3 **B**, Round 4 **A**, Round 5 **D**
Square 5: Rounds 1 & 2 **A**, Rounds 3 & 4 **B**, Round 5 **D**
Square 6: Rounds 1 & 2 **B**, Rounds 3 & 4 **C**, Round 5 **D**
Square 7: Rounds 1, 2 & 3 **B**, Round 4 **A**, Round 5 **D**
Square 8: Round 1 **B**, Round 2 **A**, Rounds 3 & 4 **C**, Round 5 **D**

continued

Seven-by-Eight Throw

THROW

Square

Ch 4, join with slip st in first ch to form a ring.

Round 1 (right side): Ch 3, 2 dc in ring, [ch 3, 3 dc in ring] 3 times, ch 3, join with a slip st in top of starting ch-3. Fasten off if changing color.

Round 2: Slip st in next 2 dc and ch-3 space or join next color with slip st in any ch-3 space, ch 3, (2 dc, ch 3, 3 dc) all in same ch-3 space, *(3 dc, ch 3, 3 dc) all in next ch-3 space; repeat from * twice, join with a slip st in top of starting ch-3. Fasten off if changing color.

Round 3: Slip st in next 2 dc and corner ch-3 space or join next color with slip st in any corner ch-3 space, ch 3, (2 dc, ch 3, 3 dc) all in same ch-3 space, *3 dc between next two 3-dc groups, (3 dc, ch 3, 3 dc) all in next corner ch-3 space; repeat from * twice, 3 dc between next two 3-dc groups, join with a slip st in top of starting ch-3. Fasten off if changing color.

Round 4: Slip st in next 2 dc and ch-3 space or join next color with slip st in any ch-3 space, ch 3, (2 dc, ch 3, 3 dc) all in same ch-3 space, *[3 dc between next two 3-dc groups] twice, (3 dc, ch 3, 3 dc) all in next corner ch-3 space, repeat from * twice, [3 dc between next two 3-dc groups] twice, join with a slip st in top of starting ch-3. Fasten off if changing color.

Round 5: Join **D** with slip st in any corner ch-3 space, ch 3, (2 dc, ch 3, 3 dc) all in same ch-3 space, *[3 dc between next two 3-dc groups] 3 times, (3 dc, ch 3, 3 dc) all in next corner ch-3 space, repeat from * twice, [3 dc between next two 3-dc groups] 3 times, join with a slip st in top of starting ch-3. Fasten off. Weave in ends.

Assembly

Arrange squares randomly. With **D**, holding right sides together, whipstitch squares into seven strips of eight squares each. Whipstitch strips together in like manner.

Border

With right side facing, join **D** with slip st in any corner ch-3 space, ch 1, *3 sc in this corner ch-3 space, sc in each dc and ch-space across to next corner ch-3 space; repeat from * around, join with a slip st in first sc. Fasten off. Weave in ends.

Nine-by-Nine Bag

Need a bag for the beach or to carry your current granny square project? This bag's squares are crocheted together as you do the last round of the squares. The benefit is you don't have to stitch all the squares together.

Easy

Finished Size
12" x 12" without handles

Red Heart® Super Saver®
2 skeins 950 Mexicana

Notions
Black cotton fabric for lining, 13" x 25"

Circular bamboo or wooden handles

Sewing needle and black sewing thread

Crochet Hook
5.0 mm (US H-8)

Gauge
First 3 rounds of square measures 3¾" across. Finished square measures 4¼" square. **CHECK YOUR GAUGE. Use any size hooks to obtain the gauge.**

BAG

Square 1

The first 3 rounds of all 18 squares are worked as follows:
Ch 4, join with slip st in first ch to form a ring.
Round 1 (right side): Ch 3, 2 dc in ring, [ch 3, 3 dc in ring] 3 times, ch 3, join with a slip st in top of starting ch-3.

Round 2: Slip st in next 2 dc and ch-3 space, ch 3, (2 dc, ch 3, 3 dc) all in same ch-3 space, *(3 dc, ch 3, 3 dc) all in next ch-3 space); repeat from * twice, join with a slip st in top of starting ch-3. Fasten off.

Round 3: Slip st in next 2 dc and corner ch 3 space, ch 3, (2 dc, ch 3, 3 dc) all in same ch-3 space, *3 dc between next two 3-dc groups, (3 dc, ch 3, 3 dc) all in next corner ch-3 space; repeat from * twice, 3 dc between next two 3-dc groups, join with a slip st in top of starting ch-3.

Round 4: Slip st in next 2 dc and corner ch-3 space, ch 1, *(sc, ch 3, sc) in corner ch-3 space, [ch 3, sc between next two 3-dc groups] twice; repeat from * 3 times, join with a slip st in first sc. Fasten off. Weave in ends.

Square 2

Work same as Square 1 through round 3.
Round 4 (1 sided joining): Slip st in next 2 dc and corner ch-3 space, ch 1, sc in corner ch-3 space, ch 1, hold Square 1 behind Square 2 with wrong sides together, slip st in corresponding corner ch-3 space on Square 1, ch 1, sc in same corner ch-3 space on Square 2, [ch 1, slip st in next ch-3 space on Square 1, ch 1, sc between next two 3-dc groups on Square 2] twice, ch 1, slip st in next ch-3 space on Square 1, ch 1, sc in corner ch-3 space on Square 2, ch 1, slip st in corner ch-3 space on Square 1, ch 1, sc in same corner ch-3 space on Square 2, now working on Square 2 only, *[ch 3, sc between next two 3-dc groups] twice, ch 3, (sc, ch 3, sc) in corner ch-3 space;

continued

Nine-by-Nine Bag

repeat from * once, [ch 3, sc between next two 3-dc groups] twice, ch 3, join with a slip st in first sc on Square 2. Fasten off.

Work and join Square 3 to Square 2 in the same manner. Work first 3 rounds of Square 4. Start second row by holding Square 4 behind Square 1 and join to top of Square 1 instead of to the side. See **Assembly Diagram**.

Square 5

Round 4 (2 sided joining): Slip st in next 2 dc and corner ch-3 space, ch 1, sc in corner ch-3 space, ch 1, hold Square 4 behind Square 5 with wrong sides together, slip st in corresponding corner ch-3 space on Square 4, ch 1, sc in same corner ch-3 space on Square 5, [ch 1, slip st in next ch-3 space on Square 4, ch 1, sc between next two 3-dc groups on Square 5] twice, ch 1, slip st in next ch-3 space on Square 4, ch 1, sc in corner ch-3 space on Square 5, slip st in corner ch-3 space on Square 4, slip st in corner ch-3 space on Square 2, ch 1, sc in same corner ch-3 space on Square 5, [ch 1, slip st in next ch-3 space on Square 2, ch 1, sc between next two 3-dc groups on Square 5] twice, ch 1, slip st in next ch-3 space on Square 2, ch 1, sc in corner ch-3 space on Square 5, ch 1, slip st in corner ch-3 space of Square 2, ch 1, sc in same corner ch-3 space of Square 5, now working on Square 5 only, [ch 3, sc between next two 3-dc groups] twice, ch 3, (sc, ch 3, sc) in corner ch-3 space, [ch 3, sc between next two 3-dc groups] twice, ch 3, join with a slip st in first sc on Square 5, fasten off.

Note

When joining squares beyond Square 5, join in same manner as previous squares substituting the number of the squares you are joining for the corresponding square numbers in the pattern numbers in the pattern.

Square 6
Using 2 sided joining, join Square 6 to Square 5 and Square 3.

Square 7
Start third row by using 1 sided joining to join Square 7 to Square 4.

Square 8
Use 2 sided joining to join Square 8 to Square 7 and Square 5.

Square 9
Use 2 sided joining to join Square 9 to Square 8 and Square 6.

Squares 10-18
Continue joining Squares in same manner as above. You will end up with a piece 3 squares wide by 6 squares high.

Fold piece in half with right sides facing. Whipstitch bottom two squares together on both sides of bag. Leave top squares unsewn on both sides. Leave bag inside-out.

Lining
Measure width of piece (it should be about 12"), add 1" for seams. Measure height of piece (it should be about 24"), add 1" for seams. You should get approximately 13" x 25". Cut a piece of fabric to this size. Press ½" seam allowance to wrong side on top and bottom so that piece now measures 13" x 24". Fold piece in half right sides together, and press. Piece now measures 13" x 12". Sew ½" side seam starting 4" from top of piece to bottom fold; repeat for other side. Press seams open. Turn lining right side out. Place inside-out bag into lining. Sew lining to bag with sewing needle and thread along top (in dc's of round 3 of squares; leaving ch-3 spaces of round 4 open to attach handle); continue sewing 4" down side, 4" up other side, along top of other side of bag, 4" down side and 4" up other side. When sewing, make sure you sew only partially through stitches so that black thread does not show on outside of bag. Turn bag right side out, so lining is inside.

Handle
Join yarn with a slip st in corner ch-3 space on top right edge of either side of bag, ch 1, sc in same space, working loosely (or stitches will not slide over bumps on handle), and holding top of one handle behind top edge of bag, insert hook through next ch-3 space and through handle, *pick up loop of yarn and draw through handle and ch-3 space, yo and draw through both loops on hook (this is a sc over the handle); repeat from * twice more in same ch-3 space, [3 sc over handle in next ch-3 space] twice, [1 sc over handle in next corner ch-3 space] twice, [3 sc over handle in next ch-3 space] 3 times, [1 sc over handle in next corner ch-3 space] twice, [3 sc over handle in next ch-3 space] 3 times, sc in last corner ch-3 space. Fasten off. Repeat for other side and other handle. Weave in ends securely.

16	17	18
13	14	15
10	11	12
7	8	9
4	5	6
1	2	3

ASSEMBLY DIAGRAM

Yarn Information

RED HEART® Super Saver® Art. E300, 100% Acrylic, available in solid color 7 oz (198 g), 364 yd (333 m); multi color, heather and print 5 oz (141 g), 244 yd (223 m); fleck 5 oz (141g), 260 yds (238 m) skeins.

Tips for Washing Super Saver

- Use gentle fabric detergent, such as Ivory®, in warm water.
- Use less than half of the suggested amount of liquid fabric softener, as too much softener will cause fiber to stretch.
- Tumble dry on low and remove from the dryer before completely dry.
- To keep fringe or pompoms looking their best, handwash, lay flat to dry.